RED ROVER

PHOENIX **POETS**

RED ROVER

SUSAN STEWART

THE UNIVERSITY OF CHICAGO PRESS
Chicago and London

SUSAN STEWART is the Annan Professor of English at Princeton University. A former MacArthur fellow, she is the author of five books of poems, most recently *Columbarium*, winner of the National Book Critics Circle award for poetry. She is also the author of many books of prose, including *Poetry and the Fate of the Senses*, winner of both the Christian Gauss award and the Truman Capote award for literary criticism, and *The Open Studio: Essays on Art and Aesthetics*. She has cotranslated Euripides' *Andromache* and *TriQuarterly 127: Contemporary Italian Poetry*, and her own poems have been translated into Italian and German. She is a member of the American Academy of Arts and Sciences and a current Chancellor of the Academy of American Poets.

Title page illustration: John Audubon, "House Wren." Male, female, and young in an old hat, nineteenth century (detail). From *The Birds of America*, v. 2, pl. 120, opp. p. 124. 26.5 x 17 cm. General Research Division, The New York Public Library, New York, New York. Photograph: The New York Public Library / Art Resource, New York.

The University of Chicago Press, Chicago 60637
The University of Chicago Press, Ltd., London
© 2008 by The University of Chicago
All rights reserved. Published 2008
Printed in the United States of America
17 16 15 14 13 12 11 10 09 08   1 2 3 4 5
ISBN-13: 978-0-226-77454-1 (cloth)
ISBN-10: 0-226-77454-6 (cloth)

Library of Congress Cataloging-in-Publication Data
Stewart, Susan (Susan A.), 1952–
    Red rover / Susan Stewart.
        p. cm. — (Phoenix poets)
    ISBN-13: 978-0-226-77454-1 (cloth : alk. paper)
    ISBN-10: 0-226-77454-6 (cloth : alk. papaer)
    I. Title
    PS3569.T474R43 2008
    811'.54—dc22   2007043806

Contents

II. THOUGHTS MADE OF METAL

III. THOUGHTS MADE OF WOOD

Acknowledgments

The following poems in this book have been previously published, often in quite different form:

The American Poetry Review: "my mother's garden," "shadowplay," "tag," "red rover," "king of the hill," "Arrowhead," "Elegy Against the Massacre at the Amish School in West Nickel Mines, Pennsylvania, Autumn 2006," "The Field of Mars as a Meadow," and "The Owl"

The Boston Review: "When I'm crying, I'm not speaking," "When I'm speaking, I'm not crying," and "The Lost Colony"

Caffeine Destiny: "Thoughts made of cloth"

Crowd: "Variations on *The Dream of the Rood*"

The Nation: "there is no natural death" (June 2007)

Poetry: "a boy's voice" and "the fox" (May 2007)

A Public Space: "The Former Age"

Raritan: "Titus," "Gold and Soil," and "Oil and Water"

Salt: "The Erl King" and "The Vision of Er," http://www.saltpublishing.com/saltmaga zine/issues/01/text/Stewart_Susan.htm

TriQuarterly: "Daylily," "Dialogue in San Clemente," and "Three Geese"

Verse: "Songs for Adam," "The Green," "Thoughts made of cloth," "Wrens," "The Complaint of Mars," "The Complaint of Venus," "Thoughts made of wood," "the sun is charity," "the window seat," "the figure in the garden," "a little room," "the rocks beneath the water," "moon at morning," "A Cone Flower," and "The Fall"

The Warwick Review (UK): "The Owl"

"A Constant State of Gravitation" and "Variations on *The Dream of the Rood*" appeared in the anthology *American Hybrid,* ed. David St. John and Cole Swenson (New York: Norton, 2008).

"moon at morning" appeared in an artist's book by Enid Mark, *The Inconstant Moon*. (Philadelphia: The Elm Press, 2007).

"Songs for Adam" was commissioned by the Chicago Symphony Orchestra for a baritone song cycle, set to music by James Primosch.

I. Spring forward, fall back

. . . the conscientious night watchman, who first carries out his duty by suppressing disturbances so that the townsmen may not be awakened . . .

The Owl

I thought somehow a piece of cloth was tossed
into the night, a piece of cloth that flew

up, then across, beyond the window.
A tablecloth or handkerchief, a knot

somehow unfolding, folded, pushing through
the thickness of the dark. I thought somehow

a piece of cloth was lost beyond the line—
released, although it seemed as if a knot

still hung, unfolding. Some human hand could not
have thrown that high, or lent such force to cloth,

and yet I knew no god would mind a square
of air so small. And still it moved and still

it swooped and disappeared beyond the pane.
The after-image went, a blot beyond

the icy glass. And, closer, there stood winter
grass so black it had no substance

until I looked again and saw it tipped
with brittle frost. An acre there (a common-

place), a line of trees, a line of stars.

So look it up: you'll find that you could lose
your sense of depth,

a leaf, a sheaf
of paper, pillow-

case, or heart-
shaped face,

a shrieking hiss,
like winds, like

death, all tangled
there in branches.

I called this poem "the owl,"
the name that, like a key, locked out the dark

and later let me close my book and sleep
a winter dream. And yet the truth remains

that I can't know just what I saw, and if
it comes each night, each dream, each star, or not

at all. It's not, it's never, evident
that waiting has no reason. The circuit of the world

belies the chaos of its forms—(the kind
of thing astronomers

look down to write
in books).

And still I thought a piece of cloth
had flown outside my window, or human hands

had freed a wing, or churning gods revealed
themselves, or, greater news, a northern owl,

a snowy owl descended.

Lavinium

I met the girl who held the flower and mirror
and the boy who sent his hoop up to the god.

Put away childish things they said, and stepped
into the future. They were made of baked earth,
their tenderness intact.

Robbers had come and gone, come
and gone for years
like glass.

In locked cabinets,
washed up: a bone brooch, the sea's
furl, an iron fire-dog.

The hoop rolled down again,
clattering.

The girl awoke and put her flower
inside the mirror.

The boy cart-wheeled
behind his wheel, end over
end, over

endless sand. We think of them.
They never think of us.
We think of them.

And the hard-hearted doll
repeated the lesson:

love's asymmetry is true,
they never think of you,

love's asymmetry is true
love's asymmetry is true

Games from Children

my mother's garden

I lost my copper key
in my mother's garden

I lost my silver knife
staring at a cloud

I found my wooden boat
hiding in the rushes

I found my wishing stone
hiding in my shoe

I lost my copper key
hiding in the rushes

I found my wooden boat
staring at a cloud

I lost my memory
when I learned to whistle

If you find my silver knife
hide it in a stone

shadowplay

I made a fist
and it grew two ears,

long ears with
a mumbling

mouth. Then
I opened my hand—

it grew
four feathers

and another hand
rose to meet it,

and two
thumbs made

a doubled
dove's beak,

curving and
nodding on

the windless
white: one four-

fingered wing
swinging out,

the other
feathering in—

blackbirds of my
bedroom wall

black birds
flying faster

than the arc
of headlights

emerging
from the road

beyond the
window, looming

and emptying
looming then

emptying
then looming

then emptying
the room of all its light.

king of the hill

What looked like a statue held a shove.
Even so, it was hard not to want
to run full throttle straight
into the arms, the very harm
of it. Some thought the figure at the top
was of another kin or kind, that only blind
force would send him over. Others swore
he would give or bend, that something like love
was standing there and could be swayed by reason
or kindness—just a push
might do him in. The view from below
was blocked by distance, and the relentless glare of the sun.

So human to feel the dominion of the sun
as a yoke, to learn that radiance can shove
a gaze back to the ground. The reason
for submission disappears: it's just part of the here below,
like thinking there's a harmless form of harm.
Time and time again, the figure up there swore
he would never relent, that it was his want
or whim to stay there, impervious to love
and hate. Our path was made straight
by that stubbornness—just a final push
we thought. But we were blind
to the outcome waiting at the top.

Once we began the game, it seemed impossible to stop
caring and turn to something else. The sun
was so hot, the voices drew us on, the crowd's blind
will bore down. Our sisters saw the harm
and called us back; our brothers swore
we couldn't go. They had felt the shove
and pull of it themselves, but forgot the way a want
grows to desire. The path was straight,
as clear as day—with a push,
they tried to lead us on to reason.
But we were planning our attack from below
and couldn't be bothered to listen to their love.

There were flowers in the meadow: buttercups and love-
lies-bleeding; milkweed pods with down bursting from their tops;
daisies by whose petals lovers swore
to love forever; and thorns left behind the leafy blind
of the thistles. Beauty was a mask for harm
and everything under the sun
had the power to draw us on or, just the same, push
us away. Does the weed also feel the deep want
of replacement, the need to go straight
for the root, then draw it out from below
there in the dark earth's hush—over
and over? Why look for a human reason

When nature has a reason
of its own? The saint said the love of a neighbor is really love
for love itself. The soul reaches out to the good. In the blind
acceptance of those about her, she makes a final push
toward the divine. Souls hover
about and above one another, in the want
of connection, promises foresworn,

and, for a time, they set all forms of harm
aside. It's vital, this straight-
forward link between them, as necessary as sun-
light or water. In such a world, the top
has no added value. The place to be is here below.

The thinker, too, looked below
the surface—to the master's power and the servant's reason.
It was the master who was blind
to history. Once he resisted the push
toward death, nothing else could harm
him. By then no more want
could arise. The servant swore
he couldn't care less, giving reality a shove.
But the truth of his work stood there in the sun-
light, steady as need and the love
of craft. The master won, though it turned out the top
was a dead end, leading straight

To oblivion. No one can escape the straight-
forward claims of the makers, the rule of the here below.
The king stands at the pleasure of those who swore
to go on and on with the game. He tells himself it's love
that keeps them swarming there in the sun
and rain, elbowing and shoving
for a closer look. But he knows what they want
is the tooth and nail of him, that the push
and prop of his image can occupy the top
for just a while. There behind the blind,
the assassin waits and has his reason—
though it's never just his own. And the worst harm

Comes from the innocents who never see the harm
at all. The crooked made straight,
the mad the font of reason,
the prophets at last gone blind.
The bloated fish rose to the top
of the stream and the rowers pushed
them down again with a shove.
The rowers were
hungry, and the sun
was in their eyes. Below
the dam, they waved their low-
bells: *what you want*

Is what you get, they said. And what we wanted
was to find the meadow, and everyone unharmed.
The farmers came running for the top,
frantic, clanging with shovel
and ax, cockamamie, heedless, straight
through the gardens, scattering the love-
nests of the larks and plovers. They swore
they would push
away the past. Their reason
was impatience swirling there below
intention. Father or son,
son and father; either way, they were blind

To the particulars and, all in all, blind
to consequence. To stop too soon is to want
to stop wanting. The hunters have their cunning reason
and go about their work by stealth. Straight
as their arrows, they aim for death, though love
is what closes the distance. Show
the trophy high on the wall, swear

to the courage of soldiers and sailors—the top
of the mast, pushed
deep into the dirt, flies a flag that declares the end of harm.
But the orphans lie sleeping in the doorways below
and will rise up, furious, with the sun.

In the end, love, there are only one or two left beneath the sun,
surrounded by silence. The blind
light blanketing the hill retreats and returns, oblivious. Love
turns the world and brings it ill or harm.
We guessed there'd be plenty and then empty straits
and both would set the whirligigging top
a-spin. We didn't need a better reason
than that to join the push
of generations. An aching want
for the future drove us on, then shoved
us back to the past. All the while, the meadow waited below.
Within the locket, it's the image our hearts wore.

We had promised, we swore
and crossed our hearts. In that sun-
flecked wood, all faith was blind.
The little boat rolled through the straits
and inlets, bent, unswerving, toward home. No other reason,
none at all. Now here below
in the something-ever-after, I've had at the top
of my thoughts a thought of love,
the shape it had before it turned to harm.
And what I've wanted
to do is to return to the source, the first push
before the fulcrum's shove.

The trail to the top
of the hill meandered. A lark hovered, shadowing the clover below,
and the hunter's blind was, in the end, abandoned. Everything that seemed
worth wanting
could slowly flower, like a weed, into harm. Still, the mind can straighten
its own path; reason has a nature sworn
to truth. A final push is waiting; its patience is a synonym for love.
The king was an idol. There's only the daylight glinting there beneath the sun.

tag

Before you touch me,
I will run.
If I touch you, you
must stop.
If I lose you, we
won't stop
and must run on
as two
forever.
Try to touch the larch's
bark, try
to call it home.
If you go beyond
the grass,
you'll have no
voice, you'll
have no one.
Beyond the grass
time stops—
try to touch
the larch's
bark, try
to touch me,

we can stop,
we can try
to call it home.

red rover

red rover, red rover,
let them come over,
red planet, red star,
attacking, attaching,
come over war against
love overcome, and come
over, red rover, let them
come over, pleaser, permitter,
decider, old teaser,
spirit moving
formless through the startled leaves.

> *come over come over*
As you stood there, shouting and waiting, shouting and waiting,
> *over come over*
> your arms linked inside
> *come over come over*
> the long shadows,

you knew the other view would come in time,

> and be like time, silent
> and waiting—

though first your name

let your own name *come over*
                    would have to tack
                              across that no man's land
           between the lines

and come over.

So when it came, in a chorus,
                sudden and strange, like
                        an offering that drew you on
                        with all its glitter,

     it hardly seemed
     it could be yours,

     and you looked around to see
     if someone else were meant.

But then you were running, running, toward them, struggling to break them or
reaching to join them.
In the end, it would turn out the same—exclusion, inclusion, small changes of
perspective.

                    That was how
                    you first met the god
                    of permissions, who has no face
                    or figure, who never
                    lingers in
                    our image.

But you didn't know that yet.

                    Someone
        would twist and fall crying

the sun dropped
vanished
            a scraped dish
a screen door's slap

and one by one

fireflies

            the mothers'
            voices lighting

calling her name

come in

then his *come in*

            and yours
            at last

you knew at once

come in come in come

in and in

though soon
in a dream again

you were running
    running toward them,
        struggling and reaching
            reaching beseeching

   if you can
   if you can't
   by a hickory limb

   the future came wearing
the look of the past

and a spirit roved restless through the shaken leaves.

Daylily

Unrecognizable now, a mash
of airy sweetness stuck
to itself, an orange stain
left on the book
where it rests. At dusk
you brought it flowering
from the ditch bank
to the desk, its
three wavy petals, three
smooth sepals—six
in all, thick
as cloth
(and each dashed
maroon above
the stem).
The stamens sprung up,
alert as antennae.
Spring dusk, dusk
for listening.

Now at dawn
an ant, determined
under-taker
(an ant as small
as a period)
makes his way like

a cursor,
diagonally,
across
the quiet
page. 1629:
A lily of a day,
Is fairer far, in May,
Although it fall, and die that night;
It was the plant, and flower of light.

Oil and Water

In your hand, a Roman votive
lamp—made of clay, like us.
Fire-floating, failing sail across
the oil, then puff,
then void.

The silent fire held back within
its well. Smallest flame in dust,
the smell of baked
earth and
bread.

Run your hand
beneath the running water,
hold it to your
lips. A word can
slip through thirst

like a wafer, like
a crumb.
A burn is cured with ice,
which makes a burn
then burn.

I knew a girl who saved a gull from death.
She gathered up its feathers gummed in tar.
She brushed the pinions down
with a toothbrush dipped
in soap, and gently
ran the faucet
on the breast.

A whale knows oil and water
and a song. This knowledge
comes from rain
and fervent
passage.

They say that oil
and water do not mix,
but one is life below
the light and one
is votive fire.

A whale knows
this, as does
a gull, as
does a girl,
now humming.

This knowledge
comes from rain
and fervent
passage.

A whale knows oil and water
and a song.

Songs for Adam

Adam lay a-bounden, bounden in a bond

I-I-I am-m-m-m a-a-a
l-l-l-likeness
without l-l-likeness.
I r-r-r-rule
the s-s-s-sea and the air.
I n-n-named a fish
and a b-bird and a stem,
and a f-f-foal by
the s-s-s-side of a m-m-mare.

My tongue was heavy, too heavy to move.
My feet were bound by roots,
but I learned to open my mouth
and sing,
to open my mouth like a bell, like
a flower.

the names

What name shall I give to thee?
What name shall I compare to thee?

anise bee and *cherry*
dark and *egg* and *free*
ghost hand and *icicle*
jinx and *kiss* and *lea*
many none and *other*
pain question row
sadness tree unusual
verity and *woe*
x I signed,
a *yawn* and *zed,*
and then I went to bed.

What name shall I give to thee?
What name shall I compare to thee?

I saw the whale shed the waves,
I saw the hawk shed the rain,
and though I was never
born, the light came first
at the limit of my mind
and with my own eyes
I could see

how all things on earth
must turn
toward the light,
though the light
has no likeness
on earth.

the dream
(four thousand winters thought he not too long)

Winter dream so sore
inside me, breath sharp
under my rib, a bent
stalk frozen
fast to another, snapped
back and lifted away,

then snow on her lashes and hair—
no, sun and dew
on her lashes,
her hair,

and the flies
buzzing in the grain

and the bees
grazing by the leaf

and the sweet dove
moaning
in the arbor.

I lifted my head to hear.

I awoke and she stood
before me, staring.
I awoke
and it all was true.

I could come upon a footprint now,
or take a turn, or find the start,

a name for something
even if it wasn't
there, was not yet
here.

the cool of the evening

Do you know every herb and seed?
he asked as he walked in the cool of the evening

(This god has intent and direction,
he knows where he's going in the cool of the evening)

Would you like to stay in the garden?
he asked as he walked in the cool of the evening

(This god has the leisure and means
to walk out alone in the cool of the evening)

There are two trees, but only one is of good and evil.
There are two trees, but only one is in the midst of the garden.
There are two trees, but only one is the tree of life.
Cherubim guard the gate and a sword
hangs crashed, hangs flailing, in flames.

Do you follow the deed with a double regret?
he asked as he walked in the cool of the evening

(This god cannot hide if he is everywhere,
he gathers his thoughts in the cool of the evening)

Cover your face with your hands and run,
cover yourselves and run.

lullabye

ashes burrs and *candlelight*
darkness endless fire
going home in
joy, I thought,
kindness leaves me now
only pity questions
rain speeds the tear
you will veer and
wander, veer and
wander…

ashes burrs and candle-
light, darkness ends
in fire, going
home in joy,
we thought, though
rain now, rain and tear.

as clerkes find written in their book

A child of my right hand
walked among the sheep
and a child of my left hand
drove the plow—

they were brothers, sons
of the self-
same mother,
no two more alike

than each other, fraught
with the pain of too little
and too much, with the pain
of too much and too little.

The god chose meat
instead of fruit
and the child
of my left hand rose up

to kill the other,
the child of my left hand,
the farmer, slew his brother,
the shepherd, in fury.

The god chose meat
instead of fruit
and the earth was stained
forever—

stained with the pain
of too little and too late,
with the pain of too late
and too little.

When you sleep in your chair
by the firelight, when you wake
in the morning and hear
the geese returning,

think of the child,
your father,
who drove the plow,
and was driven to despair,

the despair of too much
and too little,
the despair of seasons,
too little and too late.

Think of the child,
your father,
think of the mother,
your child.

The Green

Once you were grieving
         and they came to you on the white air.

They entered in
         an unending music,
                  their temple floor
                           was trodden moss.

You kept watch
         for the cleft in
                  the stone
                           that could open and
                                    close at will, like
                                             a hand.
                                                      You kept watch

through the green as it filled the white air.

Something is coming toward us,
                  consoling
                           and of another order.

It comes from a space the birds know

         (though we are just beginning)

There is something the birds know
    and sing,
        sing of
            without end.

Once you were grieving in the white air.
You thought you would not grieve like that again.

Thoughts made of cloth

satin-edged sleep,
touch down—
the braided rug
my mother wove
and wove and
wove from
her wedding
clothes.

II. Thoughts made of metal

. . . but afterward continues to do his duty by himself awakening the townsmen, if the causes of the disturbances seem to him serious and of a kind he cannot cope with alone.

The Erl King

Alder wood heaves and splits in the coppice
its white wood, cut, will bleed.

The father carries his child
before him, through darkness, chest to

chest, like a shield.
And the child hears a voice within the wind,

a voice the father cannot hear.

Who travels beside them, hovering, calling?
The child sees a shape near the saddle,

a shape the father cannot see.

The father's coat fell early and late,
the father's sigh, soft as a rag.

The child's death was what he could not grasp,
there beyond his own, beyond his strength.

Alder wood dropped in the peat will blacken,
the fossil begins where it ends.

Titus

It takes a while
to notice the star-
shaped blight
of white, flecked

red in the black
fur, a hard bite
there in the cat's
back, but it

can be inferred
from the effort
it costs him
to move first

stiffly, then
slipped like a
stripped gear
from the rug

to the sill to
the threshold
of the door
where he stops,

slinking back
from his own
motion, as if
the world there

hurts, and hurts
him—it's like
the pain the sun
brings after

a deep sleep,
at least that's
what we think,
but, too, it took

a while to notice any-
thing was wrong,
and then we
turned to stars

before we saw
the truth. And
in that time,
the time between

noticing him, the usual
cat in his usual
place on the edge
of things in

their usual places,
and noticing some-
thing terrible
had happened—

where were we,
and what do we over-
look when we say,
as we do,
that state is *bliss?*

The Former Age

A blissful life of peace and sweetness
was the life they led in the former age.
They were grateful for the fruits
that the sown fields sent them.
They were not pampered by too much.
They never heard of the grindstone or the mill.
They lived on mast, and haws, and gruel,
drinking water, cold from the well.

The ground was not wounded by the plow,
corn sprung up on its own; they ate half
the ration, not twice, as we do now.
No man knew the furrows of his land.
No man drew fire from flint.
The vine was uncut and ungathered;
no pestle ground spices
for punch bowls and roasts.

No madder, no indigo, dye or synthetic,
fleece was the color it had always been.
No killing, no pain from sword or spear,
no counterfeit coins—no coins at all.
No ship carving blue-green waves.
No salesmen loaded with kitsch.
No trumpets blasting the way to war.
No walls round and square, no towering towers.

What would have been the point of war?
There was no profit there, no riches:
Yet cursed was the time, I swear to you,
when men started their sweaty business,
grubbing up metal and lurking in the dark,
first panning for gold in the rivers.
Alas, from this came those covetous
curses that bring our present sorrow.

These tyrants are not eager to press on,
taking wilderness and deserts as their prize.
Only want is there, as the honest man said,
supplies so scarce and thin,
nothing but acorns and apples.
Wherever there is cash and the fat of the land
they will run, heedless of the law,
and batter their way with men and machines.

There were no suburban palaces and halls.
They lay in caves, in woodlands soft and sweet.
No walls walled in their blessed sleep,
the grass and leaves in perfect quiet.
They never heard of feather beds or
white-bleached sheets, and slept secure.
Their hearts were free of jealousy and spite.
Each kept faith with the other.

Hauberd and armor had never been forged.
The people were as gentle as lambs.
They had no taste for quarrels,
for each one cherished each other.
No pride, no envy, no greed.
No lord, no tyrants pressing taxes.
Humility and peace, good faith was the rule.

Neither had lustful Jupiter,
that first father of luxury,
come into this world—nor Nimrod,
ruling high from his ramparts.
Alas, alas, now may men weep and cry
for in our day there's only coveting,
double-dealing, and treason and envy.
Everywhere poison, manslaughter, and murder.

When I'm crying, I'm not speaking

Barred back from the glare
gone gripped along
the rail run down
running from or
toward no matter
no mind never
hell for leather
scraped across
night's increment
torn from the sedge
the salvage
shorn at
the edge forlorn
forewarned
hefting waxed
breached waning
whine needling
half heard
then hearing
help wound in
the wind

When I'm speaking, I'm not crying

The personal is artificially political just as
the political is artificially personal.

War profiteering has many means, including
the sale of poems against war.

Those who destroy the garden and poison
the well think that streets
will be named for them in the future.

When Aeneas, son of the goddess of love, strides out
       alone on the empty
              field, so recklessly
                     to meet the radiant killer Achilles, it's not
                     Love, but the god of earthquakes,
              who takes pity
       and lifts him, just
       in time,
right off the earth.

Meeting with slaughter, the mind breaks into parts.
Salvation hides below us and entire.

Gold and Soil

In the kingdom of the mad they mine
the earth, and the poorest of the poor
make the descent. The keepers of the coffers
keep the coffins, too, jangling as they strut
around the town.
                        Below they know
the demons of the pitch. They pray
each night to gods of flint and fire.
They fall down on their knees, and
sleep right on the ground, and wake
to bells that never see the light.
I knew a man who knew a bird
so well, the bird would come
to call him in the dawn.
He had a patch of land he scratched and fed
all day, all day until the bird sang in
the dark. The earth does not send up
its rule of law, its emissaries fume
and break apart. The bird dies first beneath
the ground, beneath
all roots, beneath all art.
Now tell me how this dream
arose, a mouth,
and came to me.

Elegy Against the Massacre at the Amish School in West Nickel Mines, Pennsylvania, Autumn 2006

Lena, Mary Liz, and Anna Mae
Marian, Naomi Rose
when time has stopped
where time has slowed
the horses wear the rain

Mary Liz, Anna Mae, Marian
Naomi Rose and Lena
the lanterns lit
at midday dark
pain's processional

Anna Mae, Marian, Naomi Rose
Lena, Mary Liz
innocence has no
argument, justice
returns in a leaf

Naomi Rose, Lena, and Mary Liz
Anna Mae and Marian
a girl is not a kind of girl
she knows her rhyme
she has her name

Lena, Naomi Rose, and Mary Liz
Marian and Anna Mae
zinnias mixed with cosmos,
lupins caught
in hay

Mary Liz, Lena, and Anna Mae
Marian, Naomi Rose
someone had a newborn
calf that died into the light,
and someone knew the night

Anna Mae, Mary Liz, and Marian
Lena and Naomi Rose
someone knew the night
holiness mere meaning
when someone knew the night

Marian, Anna Mae, Naomi
Rose, Mary Liz, and Lena
the mad put on death's
mantle, the mad
on fire with shame

Naomi Rose, Marian and Lena
Anna Mae and Mary Liz
The mother of the god you knew
was reading in her chair
and down came interruption

Naomi Rose, Lena and Marian
Mary Liz and Anne Mae
down came endless care
visitation's presence
bookmarked in a book

Anna Mae, Naomi Rose and
Mary Liz, Lena and Marian
your names in stone
your footprints kept
in mud between the stalks

Marian, Anna Mae and Lena
Naomi Rose and Mary Liz
iron bells toss
the clouds at dusk
and elders turn away

Mary Liz, Marian, Naomi
Rose, Anna Mae and Lena
empty-handed, hold their cups
with lead seams
supplicant

Lena, Mary Liz and Anna
Mae, Marian, Naomi Rose
a length of serge
so plain, so plain
the morning grass turned down

Anna Mae, Mary Liz and Marian
Lena, Naomi Rose
when time has stopped
where time has slowed
the horses wear the rain

Wrens

their tumbling joy
decanted descanting
over cobble
stones in and out
of firethorn back
and forth to gingko
who knows
who will
ever know
what net
binds them
loosening
song?
I would not
lose them
could not lose
them know
if there's
another
place another
world another life
there must be wrens.

The Lost Colony

They never learned to tell
one bird from another, a shrub

from a weedy sapling,
or when the season had

forced a flower's bloom, not
even if a berry

had ripened into poison.
And yet they drew endless

distinctions between
colors and polish and

coarseness of weave,
and would not let

their daughters
marry out.

They didn't keep
their children, though they

gave them tests and fed
them. They were known

for meticulous records, for
trophies and peeling stars.

They burned things up
or wore them down, had ranks

and staff and lecterns,
machines that moved them

from place to place, bright
jewels and playing cards.

They were old when they could
have been young, and young

when they could have been old.
They left a strange word

in a tree: *croatoan*,
and a track in the dust of Mars.

Arrowhead

Perfect flint,
we pried you up
out of the clod when
we built a hut
or dug for potatoes
at the end of summer.

You were not a fossil
leaf or chip
of bark or what
we thought,
but part of a world
drawn from rock
with rock—
sharp enough
to penetrate
fur or hide
or hated flesh,
and pin it
back to earth.

Power pulses
radiant, in and
out, out and through
the very grain
of you, from what's
persisting there
unyielding. One
small cliff-
fall backing onto
another, an exposed
spine like a hinge
sloping down
to an abyss.

Time had been honed
by a chisel
made of chisel,
pure time
aboriginal
and vanished.

What are we
doing, where are
we going,
with not a thing
to our name
the weight of this?

The Complaint of Mars

Prologue

Gray everywhere
and then a streak of red.

St. John will lead you from
the dark to leaden morning.

A sparrow sang and sang
and up the sun sprung.

And still it sang,
new vows it sung.

(I am singing, bird-wise, here
the sense of every sentence.)

And each of us is up before
the sun ransacks our beds.

Searchlights, red as row
on row, hollows warmed

in empty sheets, then
each one's solitude, each

one's sol-
itary dread.

Story

White bulls circle the morning
sky like effigies on
an urn. Fire wrings
the room of
all its joy.

Complaint

So far as my injured
mind can go, I will rehearse
my weeping—not

to ask for recompense,
only to explain
my heaviness.

I was made for certain purposes,
I gave myself over to her presence.

She is the source of openness,
of kindly lowliness, and music.

Surely she has such heaviness
from fear and woe
that, I am guessing,

in little time
her bane will be.

I have swooned and sweltered,
though I've never felt another fear.

True as metal are some,
but only the false sleep soundly.

At first bite, the fish has all he desires
and cannot know he's hooked to hurt.

A broken line, a penalty, his
wages evermore.

Complain for her who held you,
who ended all your labor.

That never did but graciousness,
please show her then some kindliness.

III. Thoughts made of wood

. . . Last night I heard the Dog-star bark,
Mars met Venus in the dark . . .

The Complaint of Venus

I

whose thrall I am, whose steadiness
and every one praises his gentleness

whose steadiness, whose thrill I am
and every one praises his gentleness

more than the mind can disguise
and every one praises his gentleness

more than the mind can guess
and every one praises his gentleness

for me to bliss and him to serve
and every one praises his gentleness

for me to serve and him to bless
and every one praises his gentleness

II

Forget to eat your supper, lie awake in bed.
Laugh while you're crying, sing while you're moaning,
Cast your eyes down, take a quick look,
Change your clothes, wipe off that smiling,
Weep in your sleep, dream while you're dancing,
All the reverse of any happiness.

Pick up the phone, twist like a rope,
Pull back the curtain, fall over the edge,
Empty your pockets, dance while you're dreaming,
A little time, a little gift, some pleasure
In the taking, some trouble in the clinging,
Some making in regretting,
All the reverse of any happiness.

Thoughts made of wood

harbor hermitage
like thrushes
twinning
hollowing grain
chaffed or
flying
a chain
a larkspur
chain or cello
hefting
a just-hatched
breathing
or bent twig
twining
branch and trunk
along runnelled
paths some
leaf-
lined paper
a sheet
a one-piece
spoon too
poor for
a bed
for newborns
in the dresser
drawer dreaming

Variations on «The Dream of the Rood»

In the wood there stood a tree and in the tree there lived a wood
that was a cross without form
      until it stood upon a hill,
      bleeding like a man
           and in the man there lived a god.

In my dream, I thought, wait—
    I can't yet
cease for a while, so midnight
        give me some
           order, some rest.

Inside me stood a dream and in the dream there was a treasure,
a chest drenched with jewels that spilled
      as slow as blood,

          unmeasured, sticky strands
          of pearls and silver
          beads along
          a vein. Along
             a vine,
                dewy strung.

If a tree speaks, it says "bear me down
                    shouldering, bear me,
                              then stand me up
                                        up like a tree again."

It says, "I was a cross in the form of a man: I was made
                    from a tree, and like a tree.
                              And I had arms like a man and
                                        was like a man,
                                                  and from the man
                                                  a god took form."

Then from his side the soul flew, sudden.
Like a cloud, the soul flew, flown.

Rust sinister, visible
          wounding from nails.
                    Endured on a hill, wracked with wires.

Wait, I thought, I can't yet cease for a while
          while a god lies, stretched, severe.
Wait, I said, I can't yet cease for a while
          while clouds fly darkly weeping,
                    while clouds fly dark as shadows flowing

I sank down, sorrow-bent
and yielding, as the talkers dismantled the god.

I was a cross from a tree, and, like a tree,
          cut down like a felled man, falling.

Like a body wet with pain, and punctured.

They cut the rock-tomb, sang the corpse cold, hewed me
            and put me in a pit
                    then found me
                            and covered my wounds
                            with silver, draped my wounds
                            with silver and gold.

Hear me, adorn me, sing me for healing.

Now I will cease for a while yet,

Joy came back with wonder born from fire

and the fire was born from the wood

    that lived within a tree

        and I dreamed beneath that tree until I woke.

Dialogue in San Clemente

Soul

When the world was too hot to touch, you carried
me into the crypt where the bulls had been slain,
a labyrinth of bricks, built
far below the teeming street.

Body

There was my match in limbo, circled
by nowhere's cloud. That was the August,
the end, of the moon's long pull
and tumult—the force of my own last hold
over you, and your first flight and dream.

Soul

Limbo was a fresco, and blameless.
You stuck me fast in the keyhole,
a speck in the eye, a splinter, this
clenching cramp, a limp, a blister—
all in all, sore and fester. Deaf
to regret, you always chide me.

Body

In truth, I rarely give you a thought;
I'm really not a drape around
a promise. You can try to fill me
with your flitting light, but I'm
water all the way through—
your shoreline at your service,
the cat's last sack, a ruin.

Soul

Pity has a swerve when it's real.
All you can think of is the climate
of your thinking, and that's not
thinking at all. Without you,
I'd be raw in the weather—
my thanks for that, I'm not complaining.

Body

If I could wander as you can,
if I could uproot and fly,
a sewer would do as a wishing
well, a mine yield stars
that shield a mine.

Soul

Little wonder there's little wonder
then. I'll wait here under
the stairs. By day I'll sweep
them up and down, by night
I'll weep beneath them.

Body

No voice, no light, are we thrown to the beasts—
or is it that they once were thrown
to us? I climbed the same stairs
and came back down, and what I saw
remains, my firmament.

Soul

What knowledge, what knowing, what knowledge—
what knowing, then, bars us from our fears?
I was glad the bright day
when we met. Will I be twice
as glad that night when we'll be parted?

A Cone Flower

Spiralling straight to the sun

Above a purple ruff like the feathers

Of a mummer
who struts down Broad Street

In terrible weather, pretending
his costume is all there is
to summer.

It doesn't matter who knows
those colors, or yours;
today, let all allusions
be local. The sun runs
its alchemy of number

And heat; the mummer naps
in his August hammock,
far from the wind and freezing
rain that, like clockwork,
fell on his parade.
There's no pity in that world—
only pattern. Behind the mask,
there's not a clue he's even

Human. It's the kind
of thing grown-ups think

children like because
it's childish, but
the children run
screaming from the room.
Beery ukeleles at a kilter,
trash bejewelling the dirty
snowbanks, glamor and
horror are buddies
for a day, boozy
under a blanket.
But never mind,

For now it does seem to be summer.
And here, in a minute, comes
the Eastern yellow-tail,
landing on the cone with
wavering wings that flare
and return—magisterial.
Today feels as if an invisible
door to an invisible
furnace has blasted
open, shimmers
of heat pulse
over and again against
the silky wings.
Meanwhile the proboscis,
sheer proliferation
of metaphor, nods
to take the nectar
one seed at a time—
little yellow-tail,
his patience
the very

Model of patience.
I had a love like that,
that started
as an inkling
of pity and grew
into a green shoot,
luxuriant leaves, and nights
and days like gardens
leading one
into the other,
mazes, amazing,
lost, and lost once more
then finally
gladly found.
It was the way
a corm or seed
can feed on darkness
in the dark, until
it becomes its own
afterthought,
a purpose no longer
bound to any purpose
and all the while
no reason for regret.
I had a love like that,
that grew in increments,
oblivious of weather,
invisible to seasons,
and it thrived beneath
the ground and
in the air—
quick as wind, quick
as light,
and lasting.

In the Western World

the sun is charity

That day the sun bore down
so fiercely coming looked like going.
We strayed, strangers in a strange part of town,
lost, past body shops and laundromats, tailors sewing
woolen hems and buttons out of season. "I am a moth,"
I thought, "I need to find a pool or, at least, a shadowed
corner, cool, near stacks of cloth."
But you were in your element, which is the glowing
blaze of noon, blinding, wherever,
whenever, your mind burns hot with impatience.
A beggar staggered toward us, "for God's sake," swaying, fevered,
and you stopped in your tracks. The light was radiance.
I would have hurried on, but for you that was the terminus.
The damp dollars, quarters, pennies, emptied without a word.
And in return no thanks, no thanks to us, no end of sun.

a boy's voice

Sometimes I catch the sound
of a boy's voice—a scrape, a scraping there, in the doubts
between what's certain. A boy's voice, bound
deep to old griefs and wonder. No wonder its roots
are hidden. You find yourself beside yourself
like a wild thing crashing
through suburban thickets, arriving all at once, helpless,
in an over-stocked backyard. Asking
or answering are the usual routes; murmuring time,
so slight, then postponed. But the boy's voice
has its music, a mixture out of crickets, pine-
cones, stones, trinkets—muffled deep in lint. A boy
with all the hours in the world, and long days I never knew,
a boy come whistling, whispering: sorely, scraped, and true.

the window seat

"Take the window seat—insist," you insist,
and now at thirty-five thousand feet, what I see
is mineral death. A salt lake, a mountain's crest
shorn flat, dust, sand, sand, dust, not a single tree
where the pale roads pale into more dust, more sand
(a cloud now and then like a stray puff from a banned
cigarette). The whole scene a triumph of vacancy.
Those intrepid wagons that landed
on the moon had four wheels made of wood,
a canvas top, a gunny sack. Some ill-formed notion of good-
ness and happiness. Guns. A crow shot out of the air.
Even so, they measured as the crow flies and spoke of days from here,
and waited for the snow to melt—
always at a loss for words, the ones for what they felt.

the figure in the garden

I

In the garden nobody sees
we leaned in heart-shaped chairs
and dropped a twig or sprig to please
the small fish circling there. A garden, a care-

less place, though who knew where or when
the math of hedge and accident had met
its happy end. We parted, and our chairs then
leaned together where we left them. A nest

and anthill came alive the moment quiet entered.
Later I returned alone, still thinking of that light,
as if the air could save the hum of every word.
But someone sat, his back to me, along the edge of trees,

a stranger, usurper, unmoved and unmoving,
stirring the wind and leaves.

II

No demon, it seems to me now,
and not an angel. He was the one in time who wrecks time,
piling up mirrors in a heap on the floor. I know
his shadow and his walk. He has all the time
in the world to stalk us, though no
designs on us. Just time taken, taking. He's timed
his entrance to meet his exit.
Sleep now, here's a cup
and pillow.
I was dreaming of a meadow,
not a garden. I thought, I remembered, just now
how I was dreaming, not of a garden,
but of a meadow.
The wind was still blowing, and you waited at the window.

a little room

If you want to kiss in an elevator
you have to know when to start.
You can't begin to bend any later
than the third floor. Your heart
is pounding (and buttons are glowing,
which means someone's waiting,
though not for you). There'll be springing,
whistling, and sudden abating,
two, then one, then two. Intent, intended,
push **>** **<** and pull me into your arms,
close and closer, suspended
(the lock switched off alarm).
Above is looming, below's the abyss—
and meanwhile the **3** is the charm.

the rocks beneath the water

Today, wandering, I could see the rocks
beneath the water, the foundation,
for the creek was clear in the clear light. The great oaks
and laurels lined the bank, their station
permanent as earth. Everyone knows that time is water
and, deeper, knows that water
erodes away all stone. But today I knew it didn't matter,
rocks or creek, creek or rocks, the slow floods
of memory, then nothing, will endure.
I remembered you at that moment
and, flowing, all the hours of since and later, immersed
in something more than monument,
and less than water—consolation
there and, in the silence, desolation.

there is no natural death

In the *Iliad*, there is no natural death—
everything comes about by intent
as if the pulse and very breath
we take were something meant
to be shaped. All that violence
out of somebody's error.
The same clumsy butting against the sense
of things over and over, horrible,
then somehow forgettable. And in the middle of the shield,
in the middle of the day, in the middle of their never-
ending tasks, the women go on yielding
to it, scrubbing the corpse cloths whiter
than ever, digging with their sticks in the dirt,
hauling the water back and forth, over
and over, where it runs forever through the dry ditch.

moon at morning

Ghostly chalk rounded low in bluest
sky, seeing, while the gulls circle
inland—lost, you think, though they know,
they must, where they're going. The women
now pinning up their washing, a tin
basin, a caboose or a tugboat, forms
of future in the distance. Found,
you think, though you couldn't say exactly
where they are. There was a place where you
were walking, though now, and now, it's fading
—it's fading, will be gone by the time
you arrive. Love there persisting
when love has almost died, when the dark it knew
has died, and still it waits, the white conscience.

the fox

Did we live lightly then?
Twice we've seen the fox,
the flash
of red that leaps
the weeds and brush, an after-
image gray,

then blank, then gone
delight cannot be sought
or pleasure thought
or joy re-caught
but twice we saw the fox, not once,
and knew his fear of us

Step in time, love, step in time,
live inside the morning
twice we saw the fox, not once,
and knew his fear of us

The Field of Mars as a Meadow

They ran with torches through the emperor's
wheat field, setting it to blaze
with a smell of burning bread,
for burning bread smells like
baked earth, as you know, and
the reason was their simple hunger.
Others came with plows, to plow it under,
and others came with stones
to cobble it over, still others came
with asphalt and tar to glue
it down, and the reason was
their need for motion.
Slaves were paraded
in triumph, in chains, through
arches built to make enemies
bow, while potsherds
and bones were thrown
to the rest, and the reason
was their need
to show their power.
The armies, public and private alike,
marched side by side
for the sake of a line
and shining mail,
hailing, conceding.
They said it was only

practice—and that
served as well
for a reason.
They sent up gifts
to the helmeted god so no one
would be struck down
by friendly fire.
The model boats were launched
on the flooded square to sail
in and out between
the statues.
Young boys came running, shouting
and whistling, women leaned
dizzily from kitchen windows,
with shutters shoved back,
cheers filled the air,
confetti fell in everyone's hair.
How long ago that was
no one remembers.
Barbarians and pirates
marauders and merchants, courtesans
and priests came and went.
The reason was the banks and
the cathedrals, and the sidereal
path of the wind.
The old streets curved into
hidden alleys, tapering
to stucco and dust.
The new ones were bulldozed
the width of tanks,
and squadrons of police
on horseback.
The reason was

to mind the mind of
the crowd, though
riots broke out in all
the piazzas. And the reason
for that was the banks,
or maybe just
the cathedrals.
When the revolution
finally ended, they
led in the cows, draped
with garlands of flowers.
Happy couples spread their picnics
here and there among the trees,
with punch and cake
to celebrate
the former age had ended.
By then my own country
started up along
a shore, impenetrable as
forests, deep
as forests.
Four walls were built
with a window facing
East, where the sun
disappeared on time
every morning,
and always returned
the next. Stories were told
in the winter dark—
of course the reason
was the need
for explanation.
Sages and prophets, as they must,

looked on ahead, and said
there would be night
before the dawn,
so they made another window,
larger, facing West,
and pushed the horizon
even farther in the distance.
The house grew lurching
wheels, and took to a road
made of sand and
mud, through
deserts, prairies and
mountains, all
the way to the sea.
Everywhere they went,
they left behind
a graveyard,
though the reason
was better left
unspoken.
Unspeakable now,
on the street below my window,
one boy is thinking of
killing another
over the five-dollar
bill that's flapping
there in his hand.
The first boy has a hidden
revolver. He found it
this morning beneath
his uncle's pillow. Or maybe
the gun found the boy.
The reason is hard to know.

Things beg to be used,
a switch tripped,
a chain hooked, a countersink
sunk into the head
of a nail.
There's a portrait on the five-spot,
a slightly cross-eyed man
(the better to have more than one
perspective), with thin lips
and large ears (the better to hear)
who looks askance each time
the bill is lifted
by the sooty
breath of the wind.
The man's the one who freed the slaves
who traveled north by stars,
who raised the generations
who raised the boys now
standing there, poised
between the not-yet
and an aftermath to come.
Floating around the emancipator's
picture are doodles and
letters, insignia and numbers,
the serial impressions of long-
gone thumbprints, specks
of lint and ink—
hieroglyphic.
A medallion hangs there
just to the left, and, inside,
an eagle smaller than a dime
spreads out his outsized wings.
A braided wreath made of laurel and wheat

makes a tiny trapeze below his claws
while he balances, clinging,
to his perch atop a shield.
Flip to the other side,
and, around the running border,
you'll find the design
of dart and egg and
dart and egg and dart and egg,
symbols of war and love for more than
two thousand years.
But no one told the boys to look,
or taught them how to glean
a sign, and no one sees them
standing there; the not-yet
still is waiting.
A dart, an eagle of the law.
An egg beside a sheaf of wheat.
Things beg to be used,
to be turned, and
the reasons to withdraw
are hard to know.

A Constant State of Gravitation

the G
is liminal / like a door

(on one side, enclosure)
on the other / eternity

the knock in the night / a fury

awakens the sleepers / unto nothing
yet (silence)

footsteps recede /
like the furious dead

to silent night
unbalanced / a jury

(or the glad all at once
into happy roar)

unbalanced / like a door

on one side receding
(on the other meeting)

like call / and response

without response (like
greeting)

like keening / like
cleaving

Gone from the glass: the ghost of a god
the guest of a chance / not yet the host.

(the lover leaned locked
outside the door

all night, all
the whole night through)

for his first need
was impediment/

and his second, limit.

The Vision of Er

When a rainbow arched behind a curtain
of sun and rain, as rainbows
always do, I thought
of the soldier, Er, who was killed
in war and then awakened, rising
from his own pyre
to tell the story.
He had spent twelve days between
the living and the dead, to return
as a messenger, he said,
to men.
He told how some souls
come up from earth,
covered
in filth and dust,
and how others come
down from heaven,
gleaming. Each one had waited
a decade of centuries—
a thousand years to be
reborn.
Suffering or glad from
penances or prizes, the souls
had their stories, too:
all that they had done
on earth

was the measure
of what was doled
to them.
And the damned were
damned forever, first greeted
by terrible roaring, then
flayed and dragged by their
feet, through thorns, to the pits
and canyons of hell
where they would stay for
yet another
thousand years.
All the while,
the Fates sang the length
of each life, casting lots
for the cycle to come.
To be greeted by silence meant
peace, and a promise
of rebirth like a shooting star.
Twelve days, eleven thousand years,
penalties paid
ten times over,
seven days in the meadow and
four days for the journey,
eight weights nested
within each other, ringing
the harmony of the spheres.
Then a clap of thunder at midnight
and a drink from the river of forgetting.
Everything structured and numbered, every-
thing set in its order. Each siren sang
one note while the whorling
weights rolled round, spinning

their colors, spangled
and white, yellow and red, and white
again—now brighter, now faster, now rimming
the limit of all that has
no limit.
And amid all this motion
and music, Er saw a sight
he found amusing and
surprising—each soul chose
the life to come
out of the life that had passed.
Orpheus asked to be born
a swan—tormented
by women, no woman's womb
would bear him.
Thamyris, the punished singer,
asked to be born as a lark.
A swan asked to sing and live
as a man, and Ajax,
bowed by humiliations,
begged to become a lion.
Agamemnon, murdered by
human hands, asked to soar
like an eagle. Atalanta, wanting
to win all her races, asked to be
turned into a boy.
The lives of all the animals
lay waiting there, too,
and every form of wealth
or deprivation, of beautiful
seeming and gesture, of virtue
and evil alike.
And no one asked

to be a number or color,
distributed over the things
of this world, no one
asked to be radiance, or
an idea in the mind of another.
Experience turned out to be destiny,
imagination bound only by reversal.
Better to be your own shadow
than something you have never
dreamed. Better to be a corpse
on earth than a sack of light
hung in the sky.
When a rainbow arched
behind a curtain
of rain and sun, as rainbows
always do,
I thought of the soldier, Er,
for he described a light
binding heaven and earth as two
rainbows spindling
about the whole, or like
ropes that bind a boat
from stem to stern.
The column of light, you see, had no name,
but the spindle was called Necessity.

The Fall

Start at the end, start at the spring,
small startling start

in the earth
the point pronged, shining
where it struck rock, fell
to the side.
I saw it, saw it shine
along the length
of the shaft—
forearm, metal
tense, feather
tufts, nock slot-
ted in the string.
Idea's mark.
Small startling
start.

I saw it, saw it shine
along the length of the shaft
over grass, over salt, past
sparrow, intending—
careless, careless
course careening,

struck then
fell, nock-
slotted,
start
small,

start at the spring,
small startling,
start.

Three Geese

snow thaw
      red haze
dusk-bent harvest
the wild geese
      vying in
one line wavering
      then fast down
close and
      closer
          thwacking
             air
      above the creek bed
one splash
      splash of
          another
             splash,
                and
                then another
glide and
gliding, three
      circles

                    rippling out
        in sequence
                swelling then receding
        on the swirling
                dark
                        water, coursing
                        fast through sliding
                                silts of snow
                March now
            thaw
            and glow silent
            out of
last light
red haze, promise
            over maples, oaks, and poplars

Notes

The epigraphs for sections one and two, "the conscientious night watchman," come from Sigmund Freud, *Dream Psychology,* trans. M. D. Eder, New York, 1920.

The epigraph for section three is from William Basse, "Tom a'Bedlam," 1653.

"Lavinium" is for Pietro Zullino.

The last four lines of "Daylily" come from Ben Jonson's "A Pindaric Ode: To the Immortal Memory and Friendship of that Noble Pair, Sir Lucius Cary and Sir H. Morison," 1629.

"Titus" is for the Wood family, to whom Titus belongs.

"The Former Age" is a translation from Chaucer's poem of the same title, ca. 1380–91.

"The Complaint of Mars" and "The Complaint of Venus" are more loosely based on Chaucer's poems by the same titles, ca. 1385–92.

"there is no natural death" is for Allen Grossman, who first brought that fact to my attention.

"The Vision of Er" is based on Plato, *Republic*, Book X, 613–21.